THE NEW FOOD GUIDE PYRAMID

Vegetables

by Emily K. Green

BLASTOFF! 2 READERS

BELLWETHER MEDIA • MINNEAPOLIS, MN

Note to Librarians, Teachers, and Parents:

Blastoff! Readers are carefully developed by literacy experts and combine standards-based content with developmentally appropriate text.

Level 1 provides the most support through repetition of high-frequency words, light text, predictable sentence patterns, and strong visual support.

Level 2 offers early readers a bit more challenge through varied simple sentences, increased text load, and less repetition of high-frequency words.

Level 3 advances early-fluent readers toward fluency through increased text and concept load, less reliance on visuals, longer sentences, and more literary language.

Whichever book is right for your reader, Blastoff! Readers are the perfect books to build confidence and encourage a love of reading that will last a lifetime!

This edition first published in 2007 by Bellwether Media.

No part of this publication may be reproduced in whole or in part without written permission of the publisher. For information regarding permission, write to Bellwether Media Inc., Attention: Permissions Department, Post Office Box 1C, Minnetonka, MN 55345-9998.

Library of Congress Cataloging-in-Publication Data
Green, Emily K., 1966–
  Vegetables / by Emily K. Green.
    p. cm. – (Blastoff! readers) (New food guide pyramid)
  Includes bibliographical references and index.
Summary: "A basic introduction to the health benefits of vegetables. Intended for kindergarten through third grade students."
  Includes bibliographical references and index.
  ISBN-10: 1-60014-002-5 (hardcover : alk. paper)
  ISBN-13: 978-1-60014-002-0 (hardcover : alk. paper)
  1. Vegetables in human nutrition–Juvenile literature. 2. Nutrition–Juvenile literature. I. Title. II. Series.

  QP144.V44G74 2007
  613.2–dc22   2006000406

Text copyright © 2007 by Bellwether Media.
Printed in the United States of America.

Table of Contents

Eating healthy foods helps
you grow strong.

The **food guide pyramid** can help you make healthy food choices.

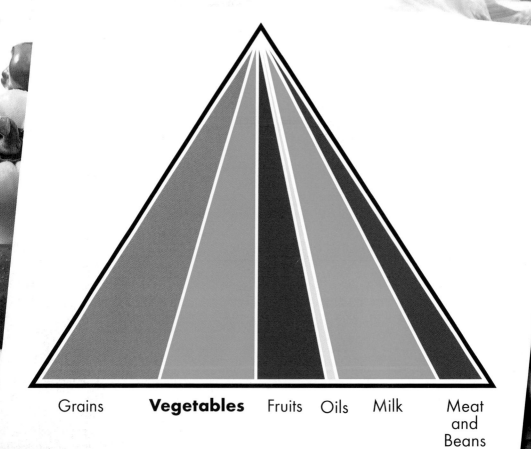

Grains **Vegetables** Fruits Oils Milk Meat and Beans

Each color on the pyramid stands for a food group. The green stripe is for vegetables.

Vegetables come in many colors and shapes.

Broccoli, tomatoes,
and peppers are in the
vegetables group.

Peas and corn are in the vegetables group.

Vegetables have **vitamins**.
Vitamin A helps keep your
eyes and skin healthy.

10

Vitamin C helps make your teeth and bones strong.

Vegetables have **fiber**. Fiber helps food move through your body.

Vitamin C helps make your teeth and bones strong.

Vegetables have **fiber**. Fiber helps food move through your body.

Fiber helps your heart
stay healthy.

2½ cups

Kids should eat about two and a half cups of vegetables every day.

Two whole carrots are
about one cup.

Eat different colored vegetables every day. Snack on vegetables with dip.

16

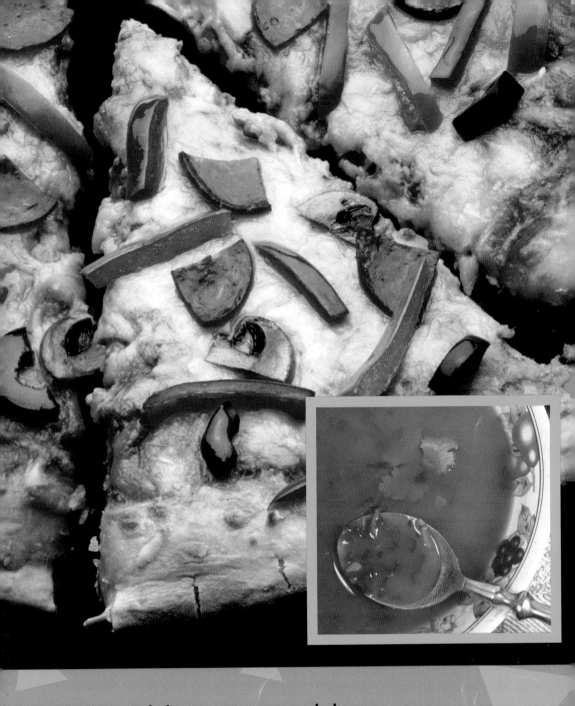

Try adding vegetables to
soup or pizza.

Don't be afraid to try a new
vegetable today.

You just might love it!

How Much Should a Kid Eat Each Day?

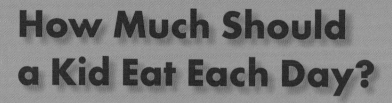

Fruits
1½ cups

Vegetables
2½ cups

Grains
6 servings

Oils
5 teaspoons

Milk, Yogurt, and Cheese
3 cups

Meat and Beans
1-2 servings

21

Glossary

fiber—the part of a plant that stays whole when it moves through your body

food guide pyramid—chart showing the kinds and amounts of foods you should eat each day

vitamins—parts of some foods that keep your body healthy

vitamin A—a part of some foods that helps to keep your eyes and skin healthy

vitamin C—a part of some foods that helps to keep your teeth and bones strong

To Learn More

AT THE LIBRARY
Blackstone, Stella and Nan Brooks. *Making Minestrone.* Cambridge, Mass.: Barefoot Books, 2000.

Leedy, Loreen. *The Edible Pyramid: Good Eating Every Day.* New York: Holiday House, 1994.

Lin, Grace. *The Ugly Vegetables.* Watertown, Mass.: Charlesbridge, 1999.

Rockwell, Lizzy. *Good Enough to Eat: A Kid's Guide To Food And Nutrition.* New York: HarperCollins, 1999.

ON THE WEB
Learning more about healthy eating is as easy as 1, 2, 3.

1. Go to www.factsurfer.com

2. Enter "healthy eating" into search box.

3. Click the "Surf" button and you will see a list of related web sites.

With factsurfer.com, finding more information is just a click away.

Index